W9-CCI-012

Shakespeare

Shakespeare

The Bard's Guide to Abuses and Affronts

RUNNING PRESS
PHILADELPHIA · LONDON

A Running Press® Miniature Edition™
© 2001 by Running Press
Illustrations © 2001 by John Lawrence
All rights reserved under the Pan-American
and International Copyright Conventions

Printed in China

Library of Congress Cataloging-in-Publication Number 2001087099

ISBN 0-7624-1103-1

This book may be ordered by mail from the publisher. Please include $1.00
for postage and handling.
But try your bookstore first!

Running Press Book Publishers
125 South Twenty-second Street
Philadelphia, Pennsylvania 19103-4399

Log onto www.specialfavors.com to order Running Press Miniature Editions™ with
your own custom-made covers!

Visit us on the web!
www.runningpress.com

Contents

Introduction

An enigmatic figure to this day, William Shakespeare is nonetheless the most studied author in the history of Western civilization. His canon includes thirty-eight plays, 154 sonnets, and two epic narrative poems, an artistic output that gained him sufficient acclaim to see his works published and sold as popular literature during his career—a privilege never before enjoyed by another playwright.

Evidently, Shakespeare garnered envy early on for his talent, but his biting wit and dexterity with insults surely had his critics running swiftly for cover. From his attacks on beauty and boorishness to his stinging critiques of character and false faith, the sheer number of affronts masterfully composed in blank verse and deftly interwoven into his dramas reveal Shakespeare's prowess as the 16th Century's leading reparteeist.

Presented here are gibes straight from the pen of the Bard himself; the insults and jabs that peppered his plays are neatly compiled into one handy volume. Even today, their sting is no less sharp than it was four hundred years ago, proving unquestionably that in any era, the pen is certainly mightier than the sword.

Beauty and Boorishness

Thou crusty
batch of nature.

—*Troilus and Cressida*

Bolting-hutch
of beastliness.

—Henry IV, Part I

I have seen better faces
in my time
than stands alone on any
shoulder that I see
before me at this instant.

—*King Lear*

The tartness
of his face
sours ripe
grapes.

—*Coriolanus*

Thou elvish-mark'd, abortive, rooting hog.

—*Richard III*

His intellect is not
replenished,
he is only an animal,
only sensible
in the duller parts.

—*Love's Labour's Lost*

Thou smell of mountain goat.

—Henry V

She is spherical,
like a globe.
I could find out
countries in her.

—*The Comedy of Errors*

When he is best,
he is a little
worse than a man,
and when he is
worst he is little
better than a beast.

—*The Merchant of Venice*

Thy mother took
into her blameful
bed some stern
untutor'd churl . . .
whose fruit thou art. . .

—*Henry VI, Part II*

Scratching could not
make it worse . . . such
a face as yours.

—*Much Ado About Nothing*

Could I come near your
beauty with my nails
I'd set my ten command-
ments in your face.

—*Henry VI, Part II*

Thou cream-
faced loon.
Where got'st that
goose look?

—*Macbeth*

There is not
ugly a fiend
of hell as thou
shalt be . . .

—*King John*

Out, you green-
sickness carrion!
Out, you baggage!
You tallow face!

—Romeo and Juliet

How ill white
hairs become a fool and
a jester! . . . So
surfeit-swell'd, so old
and so profane.

—*Henry VI, Part II*

Your breath first kindled
the dead coals of wars . . .
and brought in matter
that should feed this fire;
and now 'tis far too huge
to be blown out with
that same weak wind
which enkindled it.

—*King John*

Most smiling, smooth,
detested parasites,
courteous destroyers,
affable wolves,
meek bears . . .

—*Timon of Athens*

Out of
my sight!
Thou dost
infect
my eyes.

—Richard III

Mark the fleers, gibes and notable scorns that dwell in every region of his face.

—*Othello*

Intellect
and Speech

Hide not
thy poison
with such
sugar'd words

—*Henry VI, Par*

If thou speak'st false,
upon the next tree
shalt thou hang alive,
till famine cling thee.

—*Macbeth*

If I prove
honey-mouth'd,
let my tongue
blister.

—*The Winter's Tale*

"I know what I know."
"I can hardly believe
that, since you know not
what you speak."

—*Measure for Measure*

A fellow
of no mark
nor likelihood.

—Henry IV, Part I

My tongue will tell the anger of my heart.

—*The Taming of the Shrew*

Better a witty fool
than a foolish wit.

—*Twelfth-Night*

Your wit
makes wise
things foolish.

—*Love's Labour's Lost*

The motions
of his spirit are
as dull as night.

—*The Merchant of Venice*

I was searching
for a fool when
I found you.

—*As You Like It*

He's winding
up the watch
of his wit;
by and by
it will strike.

—*The Tempest*

Have your mouth fill'd up
before you open it.

—*Henry VIII*

You are not
worth another word.

—*Twelfth-Night*

More of your
conversation
would infect
my brain.

—*Coriolanus*

You talk
greasily,
your lips
grow foul.

—*Love's Labour's Lost*

He has not
so much brain
as ear-wax.

—*Troilus and Cressida*

There's a man hath more hair than wit.

—*The Comedy of Errors*

It is a tale told
by an idiot,
full of sound and fury,
signifying nothing.

—*Macbeth*

Your wit will not
so soon out as
another man's will;
'tis strong wedged
up in a blockhead.

—*Coriolanus*

Thou hast no more brain than I have in mine elbows.

—*Troilus and Cressida*

A false and dull-eyed fool.

—*The Merchant of Venice*

The plague
of Greece upon thee,
thou mongrel
beef-witted lord!

—*Troilus and Cressida*

Religion and Blasphemy

There is no more faith in thee than in a stewed prune.

—*Henry IV, Part I*

There is no more
mercy in him
than there is milk
in a male tiger.

—*Coriolanus*

He wears his faith but as the fashion of his hat; it ever changes with the next block.

—*Much Ado About Nothing*

A fiend like thee might
bear my soul to hell.

—*Twelfth-Night*

Get thee to a nunnery!

—*Hamlet*

Thou art
unfit for any
place but hell.

—*Richard III*

Heaven truly knows that
thou are as false as hell.

—*Othello*

An evil soul producing holy witness is like a villain with a smiling cheek, a goodly apple rotten at the heart.

—*The Merchant of Venice*

Ye have
angels' faces,
but heaven
knows
your hearts.

—*Henry VIII*

The devil hath
power to assume
a pleasing shape.

—*Hamlet*

Supposed sincere
and holy in his
thoughts . . . derives
from heaven his
quarrel and his cause.

—*Henry IV, Part II*

Thou monstrous
injurer of
heaven and earth!

—*King John*

Idol of idiot-worshippers.

—Troilus and Cressida

Earth gapes, hell burns, fiends roar, saints pray,
   To have him suddenly covey'd away.

—*Richard III*

Go to hell for an
eternal moment or so.

—*The Merry Wives of Windsor*

There's two
of you;
the devil
make a third!

—*Henry VI, Part I*

His curses
and blessings
touch me alike;
they're breath
I not believe in.

—*Henry VIII*

Chide God for making
you the
countenance you are.

—*As You Like It*

Love
and Lust

Many a good
hanging
prevents a
bad marriage.

—*Twelfth-Night*

She
adulterates
hourly.

—*King John*

. . . She's a bed-swerver.

—*The Winter's Tale*

'Tis the strumpet's plague
to beguile many
and be beguiled by one.

—*Othello*

He is given
to sports,
to wildness
and much
company.

—Julius Caesar

That kiss is comfortless as frozen water to a starved snake.

—*Titus Andronicus*

I had rather hear
my dog bark at a crow
than a man
swear he loves me.

—*Much Ado About Nothing*

O curse of marriage,
that we can call these
delicate creatures outs,
and not their appetites.

—*Othello*

I do repent the
tedious minutes I
with her have spent.

—*A Midsummer-Night's Dream*

She is ill-met
by moonlight.

—*A Midsummer-Night's Dream*

If she should make tender
of her love,
'tis very possible he'll
scorn it; for the man,
as you know all,
hath a contemptible spirit.

—*Much Ado About Nothing*

He did love her,
sir, as a gentleman
loves a woman . . .
He loved her, sir,
and loved her not.

—*All's Well that Ends Well*

Such is the simplicity of man to harken after the flesh.

—*Love's Labour's Lost*

. . . An adulterous thief,
a hypocrite, a virgin-violator.

—*Measure for Measure*

She has been
sluiced in's
absence and
his pond
fishe'd by his
next neighbour.

—*The Winter's Tale*

Being no other
but as she is,
I do not like her.

—*Much Ado About Nothing*

Character and Villainy

Thou art a wickedness.

—Twelfth-Night

Thou art a most notable coward, an infinite and endless liar, an hourly promise breaker, the owner of not one good quality.

—*All's Well that Ends Well*

In civility thou seem'st so empty.

—*As You Like It*

There's neither honesty, manhood, not good fellowship in thee.

—*Henry IV, Part I*

Are you like
the painting
of a sorrow,
a face without
a heart?

—*Hamlet*

Son and heir of a mongrel bitch.

—*King Lear*

Pernicious
blood-sucker
of sleeping men.

—*Henry VI, Part II*

Bloody, bawdy villain!
Remorseless,
treacherous, lecherous,
kindless villain!

—*Hamlet*

Such is thy audacious wickedness, thy lewd, pestiferous and dissentious pranks, as very infants prattle of thy pride.

—*Henry VI, Part I*

The villainy you teach me
I will execute,
and it shall go hard but
I will better
the instruction.

—*The Merchant of Venice*

I do hate thee
worse than a
promise-breaker.

—*Coriolanus*

You are not
worth the
dust which the
rude wind blows
in your face.

—*King Lear*

Thou are so leaky that
we much leave
thee to thy sinking.

—*Antony and Cleopatra*

Words are easy,
like the wind,
Faithful friends
are hard to find.

—*Passionate Pilgrim*

I think he be trans-
formed into a beast,
for I can no where
find him like a man.

—*As You Like It*

A fortune-teller,
a needy, hollow-eyed,
sharp-looking wretch,
a living dead man.

—*The Comedy of Errors*

His humor is lofty, his discourse
peremptory, his tongue filed,
his eye ambitious, his
gait majestical and his general
behavior vain, ridiculous,
and thrasonical. He is too
picked, too spruce, too affected,
too odd, as it were,
too peregrinate, as I may call it.

—*Love's Labour's Lost*

Bastard begot,
bastard instructed,
bastard in mind,
. . . in everything
illegitimate.

—*Troilus and Cressida*

His treasons will sit
blushing in his face.

—*Richard II*

One may
smile,
and smile,
and be
a villain.

—*Hamlet*

We make guilty of our dis-
asters the sun, the moon,
and the stars, as if we were
villains by necessity, fools
by heavenly compulsion.

—*King Lear*

One whose hard heart is buttoned up with steel . . . pitiless and rough . . .

—*The Comedy of Errors*

Thou are sick in
the world's regard,
wretched and low,
a poor unminded
outlaw sneaking home

—*Henry V*

From the extremest
upward of thy
head to the descent
and dust beneath
thy foot, a most
toad spotted traitor.

—*King Lear*

Take away this villain; shut him up.

—*Love's Labour's Lost*

I am damned in hell for swearing to gentlemen my friends, you were good soldiers and tall fellows . . .

—*The Merry Wives of Windsor*

There's neither honesty, manhood, nor good fellowship in thee.

—Henry IV, Part I

The Dramatic Works of William Shakespeare

Titles are in approximate chronological or

The First Part of King Henry VI

The Tragedy of King Richard III

Love's Labour's Lost

The Two Gentlemen of Verona

A Midsummer-Night's Dream

Romeo and Juliet

The Tragedy of Kind Richard II

The Life and Death of King John

The Merchant of Venice

The First Part of King Henry IV

The Merry Wives of Windsor

The Second Part of King Henry IV

As You Like It

The Life of King Henry V

Much Ado About Nothing

Julius Caesar

Twelfth-Night, or What You Will

Hamlet, Prince of Denmark

Troilus and Cressida

All's Well that End's Well

Measure for Measure

Othello, the Moor of Venice

King Lear

Macbeth

Antony and Cleopatra

Timon of Athens

Pericles, Prince of Tyre

Coriolanus

Cymbeline

The Winter's Tale

The Tempest

The Famous History of the Life
of King Henry VIII

127